MY ISLAND'S THE HOUSE I SLEEP IN AT NIGHT

My island's the house
I sleep in at night

Laurie Brinklow

Title: My island's the house I sleep in at night / Laurie Brinklow.
Other titles: My island is the house I sleep in at night
Names: Brinklow, Laurie, author.
Description: Poems.
ISBN 9781877010972

Cover painting *continuum* by Tasmanian artist Michaye Boulter
                              https://www.michayeboulter.com/
Photographer Julien Scheffer
Printed by Walleah Press, Trevallyn, Tasmania, Australia 7250

For the artists and writers and musicians
of Newfoundland and Tasmania
and Prince Edward Island

ACKNOWLEDGEMENTS

The spark for this book came while walking the beach at Red Point, Prince Edward Island, and pondering one of Pete Hay's observations: that Newfoundland, like Tasmania, is the psychological sink through which the mainland pours its ills. It got me thinking about two islands, on opposite sides of the planet, and how they share so many of the same attributes: roughly similar size and distance from the mainland, population, settlement origins, constitutional arrangements, and the fact that historically they have been the butt of mainland jokes. Yet both are conducive to artistic activity that seems disproportionately out of scale with the size of their populations.

While interviewing artists from Newfoundland and Tasmania, I was often struck by something my participants would say and would think, "That sounds like a poem!" The feeling happened again while transcribing the interviews, and poems just started "popping out," either as "found poems" or by weaving their words into my own poetic re-imaginings.

Excerpts of "How small an island do you need?" have appeared in Tasmania's literary journal *Island* and in Prince Edward Island's *Red Magazine*. "Rock/Shift" and "Part of the conversation" were published in *The Fiddlehead*. "The language of seashells" appeared in my 2012 collection *Here for the Music*, and is republished here with permission from The Acorn

Press. "The circumscribed geography of home" is borrowed from Wayne Johnston's novel, *The Colony of Unrequited Dreams*. Two poems in the collection, "Rock of the head" and "Everything returns, eventually," were written for two Prince Edward Islanders who figured prominently in my research; when my friends on Prince Edward Island feared that I might not return, they were my anchors. And "Everything returns, eventually" was written in response to a painting by PEI artist Susan Christensen, as part of her Frank Ledwell Literary Legacy Project. I am deeply grateful to the Vice-President Academic and Research at the University of Prince Edward Island who supported this book through a SSHRC Exchange Publication Award.

To all the people on my three favourite islands who shared their stories with me, I thank you for your words and your trust. I hope that you, dear reader, will come away from the poems feeling as much of an "islomaniac" as I am.

HOW SMALL AN ISLAND DO YOU NEED?

The first quarter-century of my life was taken up with the search for home.

I grew up in British Columbia, on the west coast of Canada. As the eldest daughter of a construction-worker dad, I spent many of my early years living in a travel trailer, moving from job to job, town to town, school to school. I felt like a turtle who carried her home on her back; I convinced myself that anywhere I was was home. By the end of grade one, I had seen the inside of four schools; by grade twelve, I had been to nineteen. By the time I was twenty I had lived in and/or travelled through five provinces and two territories. But, ironically, I had never been east of Ontario; for my family, going "down east" meant going to Peterborough, the city of my birth, to visit the relatives. Quebec was a foreign country, and, well, the Maritimes were the armpit. Only poor people and fishermen lived there. And I didn't eat fish.

For as long as I can remember we were always going to "the Island"— Vancouver Island—because the non-Ontario branch of my dad's family, including my favourite cousins, lived there. Sometimes we lived there, too, especially when my dad couldn't find a job; the Island was the place to go when we ran out of options. I remember "ferry panic" as my mom got us out the door ten hours and fifteen minutes before the six o'clock boat left, eight hundred kilometres away, and my dad going a hundred-and-twenty kilometres per hour down the Trans-Canada so we wouldn't end up being the first car in the line-up for the seven-o'clock. I remember the smell of boredom in our hot yellow station wagon: creosote from the dock pilings, sizzled tar from the pavement—and the seagulls wheeling and screeling above us. Finally rattling onto the boat, running like hooligans up the stairs from the car deck, trying to be first in the cafeteria line-up for French fries.

Precariously balancing trays while waiting impatiently for a window seat. Negotiating the lip around the table that stopped plates from hitting the floor when we hit the Georgia Strait full on. Watching the mainland fall slowly behind us and the Island loom just as slowly to greet us. Sprawling with my nose in a book across the vinyl seats, or hanging over the railing staring at our wake. My mother and father uncharacteristically relaxed and not fighting. We'd made it, and we could breathe again.

One of my earliest memories is living in a motel in Port Alberni, in 1964, just after a tidal wave from Alaska's Prince William Sound hit the Island's west coast, filling the motel swimming pool with black logs and slime before stopping just down the road from my aunt's house. The words *Vancouver Island is going to sink, you know* coming through the walls. As a kid, I didn't know about the San Andreas fault, or *the next big one.* I dreamt about driving hell-bent-for-leather to the top of a mountain with all that water rushing in behind.

I find it rather ironic thirty-eight years later to be so firmly attached to "the Island"—another island that is really just a glorified sandbar cradled in the waves just off the east coast of Canada: the tiny province of Prince Edward Island. Like most of the major turning points in my life, it was a chance left turn, in June 1983, when I was twenty-four, which led me to finding "home."

Leaving the house in London, Ontario, that gorgeous summer morning and heading out the highway to the 401, my partner and I didn't know where we were headed. *Shall we go back to the Yukon, where I have a job waiting? or Should we go visit the relatives in New Brunswick, since it is so close?* We turned left. East. Through that other country, Quebec, through picturesque fishing villages along the St. Lawrence, into northern New Brunswick, down the desolate Plaster Rock Highway into Chatham on the Miramichi River. It was while we were there that we heard that Prince Edward Island was the place to party: *You should camp at Stanhope, on the North Shore. You'll have a great time.*

About Prince Edward Island I knew only two things: Anne of Green Gables and the last name Campbell. In grade eight I had dressed up as Lucy Maud Montgomery and talked about *my* Anne books—all of which I had read voraciously. In my grade eleven social studies class in Prince George, BC, my teacher, Mr. Hannams, made us memorize all the provinces, capital cities, and premiers—and told us that *everyone* on Prince Edward Island was named Campbell (after Premier Alex Campbell). (Turns out, he was wrong: if you take a ruler to the phone book, you will soon discover that everyone is named MacDonald, Arsenault, or Gallant.)

So after two weeks of visiting the relatives in New Brunswick we packed up our newly purchased tent trailer, the truck, the black-and-white cat, and the black lab/husky cross with one brown eye and one blue eye we had brought from Whitehorse, and caught the ferry. I remember sitting in the line-up waiting for the boat at Cape Tormentine, my partner asking about the ocean: *does it freeze?* And me saying, *of course not, salt water doesn't freeze. And Anne of Green Gables, is she real?* Getting in a muddle myself: *no, she's a character in a book. But it says here in the tourist info that we must visit her house in Cavendish. Maybe it's the author's house. Then why does it say it's Anne's house?*

That first trip across the Northumberland Strait is forever etched on my retinas. The water and sky a vast cerulean canvas; on the vertical you couldn't tell where one ended and the other began. The red evening light imbuing the ochre cliffs with such intensity they seemed to glow from within. The twenty-three-shades-of-green fields like blankets flung across a sleeping child. I got off the boat and said, *This is home.*

Another quarter-century, a couple of partners, and two children later, I found myself wondering why I was so attached to the Island, why it was so emphatically "home." I realise now that the puzzle started to unravel while I was pursuing a Master of Arts in Island Studies at the University of Prince Edward Island. That the smell of creosote and cedar in the rain, the grit of sand and broken shells, sea glass and driftwood, ferry panic and campfires and sleeping on the beach under the stars on that other island had all im-printed themselves upon me. That being cocooned within a shoreline meant home. And that being an islander meant you weren't like everyone else.

Through my work at the Institute of Island Studies, I discovered that I wasn't the only one who felt this way. As part of my job as administrator of the North Atlantic Islands Programme, I had the privilege of travelling to several islands, including Iceland, the Faroe Islands, the Isle of Man, the Åland Islands, Cape Breton Island, and Newfoundland. We also hosted conferences, where dozens of islanders came to us. What was the common bond that made them talk at these conferences: from the moment they got off the ferry or the plane until they got back on several days later? What was it about islands that was so special?

In 2010 I travelled to Tasmania to undertake doctoral studies with Dr. Pete Hay in the University of Tasmania's School of Geography and Environmental Studies. Analysing artistic expression of Newfoundland and Tasmanian culture and the words of their creators, I explored the inspirations and stories behind the art, the extent to which attachment to place, island identity, and the prevalence of story (the "glue" that binds people to their place) play a role in islanders' perceptions of self, individually and collectively. On these islands, artists possess a cultural confidence that comes from maintaining their distinctiveness.

In asking that question now, I have had remarkably similar responses, whether the person is island-born or -bred, or whether he or she came as a teenager or adult. When I talk to them about the concept of "islandness," nearly everyone gets a far-off look in their eyes as they start to think about it. And then the conversation begins: *I grew up here, but moved away to go to school. And now I'm back. Now that I think about it, we always go to an island for our vacation. When I go to an island, I need to climb to the highest point. I find that I can't live away from the ocean.* Although a few look at me quizzically and wonder what all the fuss is about. Or they tell me they have never thought about it before: the little patch of ground they live upon is simply "home."

For those who *choose* to come to an island, some come to escape failed relationships or a meddling family, describing it, as one friend calls it, as a "time-out." A time-out from messiness on the mainland; a time to downsize, to regroup, and reorder; a time to put things back in boxes, with boundaries. Life can fit neatly once again within what Prince Edward Island poet Milton Acorn calls "the wave-lined edge of home." Others choose to come for the lifestyle—it never takes long to get anywhere, and rush hour is rush hour in paradise, but more usually rush minute. So many people say they came for six months, or three, or just a holiday, and here they are still, years later. Some felt they had no choice: they were captured.

For some, living on an island is a symbol of their search for simplicity, to get back to what it means to "be" instead of "do." It gives meaning in a meaningless world, place when you are mired in placelessness, distinctiveness in a world of bland. Islands, with their mesmerizing soundscapes and seascapes, the unrelenting changeability of tide and wind, their landscapes laid bare, capture people's imaginations: we write about them, make songs and art and movies about them, and vacation on them. But for all their apparent simplicity, there is an intensity to island life—it is distilled, pared down to the essentials.

Being on an island is about physical, psychological, and social boundedness, in many senses of the word. Geographically, a strait or other body of water delineating an island is an emphatic and simultaneously shifting barrier. Unlike a border, say, between two provinces or states where it may feel just the same on one side of the "imaginary" line as it does on the other (if you even know or notice you have crossed it), you have to make a conscious decision to get to an island—or indeed to leave it. A water boundary provides a tangible separation between what you are leaving behind and what you are heading towards. When Northumberland Bridge Builders built the 12.9-kilometre Confederation Bridge to Prince Edward Island in 1997, what many people missed most thereafter was the ferry ride. Gone was that "in-betweenness" when you were neither here nor there, when you could catch your breath and savour time to yourself, or you could check out the lounges to see if you knew anyone to go have coffee with—and invariably you would.

On islands there is a psychological boundedness, too. We all know the phrase from John Donne's meditation, "No man is an island." Yet many of us *are* islands— island*ed*—and some of us are more so than others. Just how much you let in or out depends on the tides, the shore, your own personal boundaries. Think of all those stoics we know, who reveal little. At the same time, a small island is knowable. You can get your arms and your head around it. An island is not something apart from you, but is something you can be a part of. You can live your life with certainty knowing where your edges are. For some people, an island is not an island unless you can go to its highest point and see the water all around. For others, you know that if you keep walking you will come to the edge eventually. For some, knowing that after the ferry stops running at night, who's on the island is on it, and who's not is not. For others, it's the way the light falls on the trees or the intensity of the rainbows, the way the fog rolls in over the bay or the rain comes down sideways, or the way the clothes snap on the clothesline or the woodpiles are stacked.

Then there are societal bounds. If you are open, islanders will take you in. Just as the island can give you what you need, the island is open to what you give it. You can make a difference on an island; it is easy to become a big fish in a little pond. You might have to listen to the jokes of having to be seven generations born and bred before you're a "real" islander (this idea ignores 13,000 years of Aboriginal presence). But you can take solace in the fact that the erratics that came with the ice age are considered "from away," too. You learn to live within family and societal rules, getting along with other islanders in a small bounded space—spoken but mostly unspoken—relation*ships* navigating murky waters. However, some come-from-aways or "blow-ins" never fit in, or they find the in-your-facedness, the parochialism, intolerable. They're usually miserable, and most of them leave.

After a while, to live on an island can become a badge of honour. You're proud that you're a little "out there," that maybe you have to work a little harder in order to survive. Islanders are a resilient lot, which can come from having to cope with and adapt to the harshest of the elements, the isolation, occasionally having the mainland cut off again. Islands are small enough to adapt quickly to change. They can turn on a dime, meaning they can be a laboratory for change. They can also be the canary in the coal mine, what have been called "environmental and cultural bellwethers," harbingers of what is to come on a global scale.

Someone told me once that *islands are places mainland people forget.* It is easy to get huffy when mainlanders forget to include you on the map. First you get defensive, then you get downright annoyed. Then you realise it is probably just as well—it is getting kind of crowded and you don't want them here anyway. And some islanders, such as those in Newfoundland, are known for their sense of humour— Newfoundlanders have an indomitable spirit that comes from being seen as the underdog when they know that they're not. Rumour has it that they started the Newfie jokes that are told on the mainland. And then there are the two-headed Tassie jokes. Tasmanians probably plant them to keep people away: *don't tell anyone what Tasmania is really like, or everyone will want to live here.*

And if you were born on an island, you are already ahead of the game. You may spend your childhood waiting to leave, but after a while you find yourself jumping at the first chance to come back. Places have a way of imprinting themselves on you, especially when you are young, but it can happen when you are older, too. That place where you've had particularly moving experiences helps you define who you are, becomes part of your identity. Because life on an island is often distilled, concentrated, islandness focuses people's attachment to place. Because the island is bounded, defined against a larger mainland, islanders sometimes feel as if they are a people apart—something about being the underdog, that you have worked just a little harder to get there, or survive there. And from the island you can orient yourself to the world.

To become an islander is to know in your bones that you are home. I set down roots in this fertile red soil where my children were conceived and born. My memories are of skating with them on winter ponds, paddling with them along the shoreline, throwing sticks for our golden retriever along the Confederation Trail that runs the length of the island, watching the movement of the marram grass answer the wind and the sea grass answer the tide, walking the red-sand shore and building sand castles, and seeing the sun set at Brackley Beach—they are all part of who I am on my island. Its story is my story. If place is the ground in which we plant ourselves with firmness and conviction, then it stands to reason that the smaller the place the more solid it is in relation to our consciousness: you can hold it in your head—and your heart. On an island you can *see* with your eyes just *where* you are, and what your limits are. And this might give you a better per-spective on the world. The island as metaphor for the self; the island as the perfect little poem.

I

THE CIRCUMSCRIBED GEOGRAPHY OF HOME

THE LANGUAGE OF SEASHELLS

for Pete Hay

I know seashells, you say
as you walk Nebraska Beach
head down
hands behind back

The vernacular names, anyway
painted ladies, flower cones, doughboys
cart-ruts, hairy arks

It was simple, you say
I'd pick up something beautiful
and want to know what it was

A man who knows his place
on an island off an island
at the edge of the end of the world

Where the sea writes its story
on dolerite and mudstone
revealing the lines and the distances
between blood and carbon, breathing and not

Where the absences make you ache
and you're forever reminded of them
as you walk the bush or shore

Where the tragedy, you say
is not that our young people leave
but that they don't come back

Just up ahead you catch movement on the cliff
a blackfella caught in the Black Line?
a thylacine extinct?
a child long gone?

But it was only the light
a reminder of what's missing
and what's here

Back from the beach
you add a warty rock-whelk to your shelf
brush off the grit of a thousand years of waves
on rock and bone and glass and shell

Out the corner of your eye
the glimpse you carry
like sand trapped
in the seams of your pockets

Tasmania's Pete Hay is a poet and essayist, a teacher, an environmental philosopher, and one of the world's foremost thinkers on/with islands and islandness.

DEEP SPACE

for John Steffler

You went out alone to the Grey Islands
but went in, too
to the ghost place where you
tripped over threads of stories
saw what a human life is capable of
what it needs to survive in this place

confronted loss
as people left ancestors behind
floated their houses
or hauled them over the ice
to their new home
on the mainland

The most recent newcomer, yet
the oldest forefather, you were
like one of those Irish workers sent out
by the fishing companies to make salt fish in the summers
and then go back to Kinsale or wherever

and later stayed
to fish and build outport lives and boats
that bound them
to the Old World, the Caribbean, and beyond

Like the guy in Harbour Deep
whose father built a schooner
And this man used to say
time to go to Spain and get some more salt

The ocean connecting people down through the centuries
yet a chaos, too
Living near the ocean, or living off the ocean
trying to make a living from it

has a profound influence on people's sense
of what they can own
and possess and preserve

No one can own the sea
You can assign fishing grounds, make nautical charts
but you can't walk around on it, you can't fence it

The land rarely rears up and smashes your house
wrecks your garage or barn
but the sea does that regularly
sweeps away wharfs and breaks up boats

In the world I grew up in
people could at least pretend
they were more protected from the vagaries of existence
but here there's no hiding

Being on the edge of the sea
is like looking from the edge of the earth
into outer space

Late-night CBC newscasts
weave in and out the shortwave
words furl into the sleeping bag
you hold tight to your chin
curl around ancestral whispers
that mingle with late-night notes
of a piano sonata
your conduit to the universe

It's how I imagine Mozart would sound
to someone in a space capsule
orbiting the earth

or maybe drifting into deep outer space

part of the unscripted dance you were called to find
there on the Grey Islands

Things in yourself might be as surprising
as things you encounter outside yourself
a two-way discovery
of what's in
and what's out
there

John Steffler grew up in Ontario and moved to Corner Brook, NL, to teach English at Memorial University's Grenfell Campus. An award-winning novelist and poet, he has served as the Canadian Parliamentary Poet Laureate. He lives once again in rural Ontario. His most recent book of poetry is And Yet.

GODDESS OF SMALL THINGS
for Rees Campbell

You tell me about the argonaut
tiny and translucent clinging to its shell
its eye contracting from the light of your torch
but without enough life to hold on
it flopped out

leaving you with the holy grail of shells
moonlight trapped
in the life force
of shimmer

But at what cost?
Knowing there is no gift from nature
that doesn't extract a price

What cost to this island
are the poems you write now
"The last Tasmanian devil died today"
"Tasmanian Shore Bird Count 2010"

The shells you collect
often cracked and chipped
because that's how they should be
If you find them like that
they have been used for their purpose
You don't need to kill for that

Like the people we killed to make our place here
Woolnorth Point
known by the black community as Massacre Bay
and the white community as Suicide Bay
the impossible choice
to be shot
or to leap off a cliff into a raging sea

You are the island's conscience

You see the small things
in the infiniteness of nature
like the paper nautilus shell
found in the wash of a windstormy night
on White Night Beach, Flinders Island

each of those things an encapsulated world
one within the other

Rees Campbell is an educator, writer, and poet who lives in northern Tasmania.

WALK WITH ME ON SKULLBONE PLAINS

for Richie, Matt, and Pete

The Palawa people told me that the land's stories come up to you through your feet.
—RICHARD FLANAGAN

walk with me on Skullbone Plains
where blue-wash sky wraps
you in silk traps
you to reveal
the bones of earth laid bare

where coral lichen enshrouds
you in lacy sheets clouds
the hillbound plain
narrowing your view

take off your shoes
step light across my back
feel my storysong pulse up through
your feet, knees, and hands

to fingers that touch
my soft cushion cheeks
and run
through my grey lichen hair
to your mouth that drinks
my water clear and cold
let it run through your veins
so that I am in you
just as you are in me

don't let the barnacled skulls
of the fallen giants who came before
scare you
don't let the bones of their offerings
fool you

into thinking that you are just another suitor
who has come to be my saviour

know that beneath the mounds of ochre and olive
they too have uncovered my secrets
they too have walked my story
they too sleep alongside me
on Skullbone Plains

Richie Wastell is a painter, Matthew Newton a documentary photographer, and Pete Hay a poet, all from Tasmania.

2

THE ROTE OF THE SEA

ALWAYS LEAVING

for Michaye Boulter

The sea your road
the hole in the sky
your light to travel by

You learn to climb before you can walk
swim before you can talk the language
of wind that lures you to shore
then makes you leave again

You learn down by the tilt of the deck
up by the lilt of the stars
numbers by counting the whites of the waves
and colours by tracing the edges of clouds

Bleeding the hundred shades
of blue across your canvas
that is your leaving now

Today the sky a curtain you paint
to see what lies behind

*Having spent most of her life on the ocean—sailing and living on an island—Tasmanian
visual artist Michaye Boulter takes her inspiration from the sea.*

LISA'S SENSE OF WATER

for Lisa Moore

Summers around the bay
there's a different sense of time
enough quiet to settle
dig deep

North Atlantic swells pound her senses
how the sea works frightens her
the power, the mystery
the unimaginability of eighty-four men
dying out there with nothing

But she takes it as it is
Of course, I didn't write that story, she says
I wrote a shadow of that story

She'd like to be unfettered by notions
of nationalism or political affiliations
or even a sense of belonging

She'd like to step into the skin of anyone
anywhere or any place

But, as she ages, her body connects her to place
The concrete and the imagined—
how they inform each other, yes?

She knows there are stories
left to be written

Swimming in the North Atlantic she recognizes the pull

Lisa Moore is a Newfoundland writer. Her books include Alligator, Open, Caught, Something for Everyone, *and the award-winning novel* February, *about the sinking of the* Ocean Ranger *oil rig in 1982.*

BEACH EARS

for John Cameron

Your love of water began
when your mother took you to the shore
Beeline to the sea on little toddler legs
She'd have to fish you out

There's this great physical yearning to immerse myself
all the way down to the bones

Now you find yourself at Blackstone
across the channel on North Bruny Island
where changeability is light play on water
a metaphor that runs more deeply

    molten lead lapping, *shh shh*

When I come out on the verandah
I feel different inside myself
leave my logical mind at the door
and open my heart
Only then can I begin to learn
the language of the rock

We walk the path to the shore
Halfway down
you point out the difference
the sound of the waves gets louder
bush tang to the wind is gone
A lapwing lets everybody know
that a couple of humans are coming down

    green copper nudging, *shh shh*

You show me sea-green lines
indentations that look like carvings

See that white eye
like a dragon coming out of the rock?
Guardian of the shoreline

I ask about the footprints
that led me to your door
Etched in ochre sandstone
they look a bit like beach ears

feeding on minerals, *shh shh*

You tell me it's the salt air and water
that push the iron out in circles
and as the salt crystals get in
and the sand grains swell up
we get bulbous mushrooms

But what look like solid structures
you can see are coming adrift
And all these holes that used to hold mushrooms?
I think they are your beach ears

The coastal geomorphology
you thought was ancient
(240 million years, give or take)
turns out to be relatively recent

These giant footsteps running to the water
are the ecological footprint that tell me
the sea level is rising and the shore is eroding

and the land is always listening
pewter, grey and malleable, *shh shh*
here comes the water

Retired social ecology professor and place phenomenologist John Cameron grew up in Australia and now
lives in Hobart, Tasmania.

ROCK/SHIFT

for Don McKay

The oldest continental rocks in Newfoundland and Labrador are 3,800 million years old,
but the oldest rocks in the ocean are only 150 million years old.

  —Newfoundland and Labrador: Traveller's Guide to the Geology

When you plug in deep time
everything becomes more complicated

A member of the clan come-from-away
you say you don't want to be anything else
On Newfoundland, everything is from away
Even the rock that comes from Gondwana, Avalonia, Laurentia
all jammed together to make this isle
stuck out in the Labrador Current

Other places we know
were where they are
but here, you say, *we are all new*

The traces in the rock remind us
even the light trapped in the Labradorite
comes from away
So you fit right in

Just the first baby step back and that erases us

Oil workers, miners, sealers, sailors
soldiers, fishermen
Beothuk
who did not have to die

Perception shifts
when you first come to this island
All the communities seem so close together

The longer you live here
the farther apart

Hank Williams,
Dr. H. Williams, the geologist
used to call it
the holy ground of plate tectonics

And after the ocean has worn the rock away
even the shadow of our bones will be gone

Don McKay is an award-winning poet who lives in St. John's, NL. His book Strike/Slip *won the Griffin Poetry Prize in 2006 and he has twice won the Governor General's Award for Poetry, for* Night Field *in 1991 and* Another Gravity *in 2000.*

3

AN ISLAND STORYBOOK

NECKLACE FOR THE SAWYER'S WIFE
for Vicki King

Before Blackstone
you planted English gardens
and reaped what you sowed in paint

In time your palette washed out
drained itself of colour
narrowed to a single brushstroke of dun
the colour of the earth-
line that led you here to Bruny Island
on the D'Entrecasteaux Channel

Taking pictures by canoe you followed a heron round the point
FOR SALE on Blackstone Bay a sign

for fifty clapped-out acres
and a house looking out the channel that brings you
twists of history in rope and net
memories etched in driftwood and glass, bone
peeled, wizened, worn

and the story of sawyers rowing two black men and with Truganini watching
the sawyers push them over the side and when they reach out for help the
sawyers chop off their hands then rape her over and over as her husband-
who-would-have-been sinks beneath the skin of water
flesh of sky

The land gives up its stories, too
where thistles choke out pasture
bleached skeletons of wallabies and sheep
caught in barbed-wire fencing
rusted harrows and discs and wire
where burnt-out grass-trees shake their angry manes
at the sod hut George Augustus Robinson built
to launch his Friendly Mission

to relocate the Aborigines to camps to starve

Hanging up your brushes
you jumble your sheds with wood and metal and glass
that you piece together to voice this place
Your tools a Stanley knife
a saw and a hand
drill for holes
to thread the wire through

You bend barbed wire into fingers
gnarl the points into knuckle joints
hang hands from a leg-iron chain to make
a necklace for the sawyer's wife

Victoria King is a painter, sculptor, and writer who found Bruny Island, Tasmania, to be a particularly inspiring place to live and make art. She now lives in Manchester, UK.

THAT *THING*

for Michael Crummey

If Newfoundland were a thing
you'd give it to me
You're just that kind of guy

You'd give me hi's and how-the-hell-are-ya's
invite me home, open your fridge
say, *take what's there, it's yours*

You'd give me that little place in Western Bay
where your dad grew up
and the whole coast of Gros Morne

You say you feel a bit ridiculous saying that
that you could just give a coast away
but it's so spectacular
so much a part of who I am
that it belongs to me
in a way nowhere else does

You'd give me what being an islander feels like
not so much the sense of water
but what the water does
and what the water brings
fish and driftwood, bodies and weather
that urge to come home
to be home
that *thing*

And you'd give me stories
Or maybe even the antenna you inherited from your dad
the one that picked up the stories
filling in the static with *your* words and *your* images
so that we can feel it, too

Giving it away is what you do
not caring that in the giving
you get back a thousandfold
That's not why you do it

You just do

Michael Crummey is an award-winning novelist and poet who lives in St. John's, NL. Books include Hard Light, Galore, Sweetland, *and* The Innocents.

WAYNE JOHNSTON TALKS ABOUT THE WEATHER
for Wayne Johnston

When I was a kid
we had two channels in Newfoundland: CBC and CTV.

I come from an anti-confederate family,
so we weren't allowed to watch CBC.
That was the Canadian channel.

On CTV there was a weatherman named Bob Lewis.
And he'd do the weather.
And he would always get it wrong.
But it wasn't his fault.
It was nobody's fault.
Aside from fortune-tellers,
there are people who can predict the stock market
and people who can predict the weather.
Weather's hard to predict, you know?

When you look at the weather map on TV
and see a low in, say, New York or Boston,
that's tomorrow in Newfoundland.

That's how I thought about it.
We were getting everybody else's used weather.
It was being handed down to us.

Time and space were linked like that map.
I knew that weather moved from west to east.
And time was moving west to east.
Time was moving toward the island.

*

There are two animating myths of Newfoundland.
One is that we're better than everyone else,

and the other is that we're worse than everyone else,
getting everyone else's hand-me-downs.
It's like you take a certain pride
in coming from a small remote place.
Yet if anyone criticizes or makes fun,
there's this fierce sense of grievance.

Two warring aspects
in the same collective mind.

*

I never separate Catholicism
from growing up in Newfoundland.
If you come to Newfoundland as a grown-up
it's like converting to Catholicism as a grown-up.

The whole idea of Catholic guilt, you know?
And the notion that there's one place you can go
to tell a secret of a certain sort?
Irish families tend to have secrets.

When I was growing up,
to take confession as you were invited to take it,
admit to doing anything wrong,
you were considered pretty naïve.

On many occasions I've seen
any sort of credulous boys
go into a confessional
own up to something
and the priest would come out
yank open the door
and beat the living daylights out of him.

That was your penance then.
Not ten Hail Mary's.
Not ten Our Fathers.
But ten cuffs to the back of the head.
I come from a long line of liars.

*

You know that song,
"Thank God we're surrounded by water"?

I really don't like being surrounded by water.

To tell you the truth,
I've never liked the ocean.
You know how they used to talk about computers
not being user-friendly?
That's how I feel about the ocean.

All you could do was look at it.
It was too damn cold to swim in.
And there was no other side to it.
It didn't seem to lead anywhere.

I used to think there was no more forlorn a sight
than to see a ship leave St. John's Harbour
all alone at twilight
and head out into that nebulous elsewhere.

Wayne Johnston is an award-winning Newfoundland writer who lives in Toronto. Novels include Colony of Unrequited Dreams, The Custodian of Paradise, The Son of a Certain Woman, *and* First Snow, Last Light.

IF TIME SHOULD LAST

for Bernice Morgan

She remembers the day and the smell
as if it were yesterday

Wartime and the train from St. John's to Clarenville
a large boat from Gambo to someplace else
a smaller boat to the Cape

Just a spit of land
but a playground for three meek
bare-kneed city kids
who had never been outside the garden
without their parents
dropped down on the beach
where their mother used to walk barefoot

My mother would talk about sitting on the wharf
dangling her feet
playing with pieces of shells
bits of dishes and broken concrete all smooth from the sea
There was sand and there were gardens
and everyone grew everything
just like heaven

But then the wells became salt
and they moved into town
her grandmother round the corner on Merrymeeting Road
Listened to them talk about where they came from
how nothing bad ever happened in the Cape

Yet the ocean was a constant threat
You knew you were taking a chance
and every year, someone died
More than one, many years
No doctor, no electricity, no roads

Blocked most of the year by ice
Black dark, black dark
You cannot imagine the blackness
until you go to a Newfoundland outport

Beyond the dark breeds myth and possibility
My mother's uncle always thought people
were watching them
Like sometimes if you went for a walk
you could see lights in the marshes and bogs
It's not hard to imagine the unnatural
if you're cut off from the outside world

If she's not near the sea
it's like a room with no doors
From her bedroom she looks out to the narrows

Some mornings you see a line out there that looks like ice
all glittering white with the sun and the reflection of snow
I don't think it ever freezes over anymore

Just like when she goes for a walk now
and says *I'll meet you up by the Paramount*
and the Paramount's not there
It's an office building that used to be called
the Paramount. We're always using landmarks
in a city that's not there
Your St. John's is not my St. John's

My grandmother used to say
Oh, I'll come in to see you next week if time should last
Did it mean that the world would stop?
Or just time?

Bernice Morgan was born and raised in St. John's. She is the author of Cloud of Bone, *and* Random Passage *and* Waiting for Time, *which were made into a TV mini-series.*

AURORA BOREALIS

for Don McKay

Spirit beings of aurora borealis, say the Inuit, remain trapped in the rock, still dancing the dancerless dance.

—DON McKAY, "Labradorite"

We thought she was dead. Buried
in the weight of millennia
pressing down from above
Lost in deep time
beyond hope, longing, or even despair

But even rock can't withstand
the pressure. Cracks appear
fissures that deepen with heat
and cold, freezing and thawing
of each passing orbit

And the sun is persistent
always seeking, always yearning
until one day she finds her sister
seemingly dead to the touch
no longer of this world
or the next

Sun nudges her way
in, filling the cracks
until, stirring, unfurling
Aurora hauls herself up and out

and in one electric motion
erupts, spills
molten joy encircling the sky
dancing with the ancestors
at the ends of the world

TOO MANY STORIES

for Carol Penton

Ironic you should ask
how many generations I am.
I was born in Coachman's Cove
on the Baie Verte Peninsula.
I was a Walsh, Caroline Walsh.
I had Irish roots,
so when they adopted me,
brought me here to Joe Batt's Arm,
I just slid right in.

My mother was diagnosed with cervical cancer
a couple years later. Sent away to St. John's.
I moved in with my grandmother and grandfather Becker
who were old even back then.
Island living, it keeps you close.

I remember one night in the old house,
the window right here faced the ocean,
it just had the four panes of glass,
and my grandfather standing with his rosary beads
in his one-piece underwear
and he's watching through the window
because my uncles weren't home.
And he's praying for my mother
who was having surgery after surgery after surgery.

And the words in the rosaries were strong,
Sacred heart of Jesus, have pity on the dying.
Even the non-Catholics would come in and kneel down with us.
But she didn't die.
When she was leaving the hospital, the nurses said,
If you had started studying your RN when you came in,
you'd be graduating now.

*

I had two bachelor uncles.
They would go fishing every single morning.
Our house was right by the ocean
just like most of the houses here.
I was an adventurous type,
I just wanted to play by the water.
But everybody was terrified,
waiting for me to slip on some kelp and fall in.
My Uncle Anthony was a real drama king.
At the supper table he says,
Saw that shark again today, Mother.
And of course my ears just perked.

Oh, you did?

Yup, the shark came up the side of the boat and said,
Do you know Carol Penton?
And I said, Yes.

I want to eat her for my supper!

Scarred for life!
People don't realize
they did what they had to do
to keep me safe.

*

Can you imagine having the opportunity
to walk back into that era?
Walking into the old houses, the old wallpaper.
The floor canvas was like big flowers, bright colours,
the old table with the spindly legs.
My mother, God rest her soul,

would always say how hungry they were
in the spring, before the seals,
how much she loved pan-fried ribs,
stewed flipper with paste,
their own vegetables from the cellar,
how delectable that would be
when that feed of seal would come.
It's gotta be hard for my seventeen-year-old,
or any seventeen-year-old,
to comprehend
somebody belonging to them
being that hungry.

*

I loves where I'm from.
When Joey Smallwood stood
on the tailgate of someone's truck
up by the Fogo Island Motel where the hospital is now
they threw rocks, booed, yelled,
How dare you tell us we have to leave!
Too much water had passed under the bridge
too many people buried in the cemeteries
too many people struggled to survive
too many nights sitting around a kitchen with the lantern lit,
doing your homework, using home-made bread for your eraser.

Too many stories were told,
stories that must have been sprinkled with fairy dust
because they continue on.
Thank God for them.
They saved us.

Carol Penton was the long-time editor of the newspaper, The Fogo Island Flame.

4

HOW TO PAINT AN ISLAND

OLD SHAREMEN

for Winston Osmond

Here at the end of Herring Cove Road, Shoal Bay, Fogo Island
fishing's like breathing
your people can't give it up

It's something born into them
even though you say
and I don't care who hears this
the fishery never was, and never will be
a good living

You went to Toronto
like everyone did, then Alberta
Faro Mine in the Yukon
but home nagged
the elastic band hauls you back all the time
I knew that if I stayed there this long
I would have this much money
and be this happy
Or I can go home and be this happy
broke

Here at the end of Herring Cove Road, Shoal Bay, Fogo Island
this island is yours, you carry it in your head
not like the mainland, too big to own
that to me is like a bird in a cage

Here at the end of Herring Cove Road, Shoal Bay, Fogo Island
the water's your playground, your clock
We got up
and like ducks went to the water
even the smallest one crawled

Here at the end of Herring Cove Road, Shoal Bay, Fogo Island
the tide your calendar, marks your days, weeks and months

The seagulls told us when winter was over
the 29th of March, the gulls would come back
the 28th of June, the terns
And with the terns there was salmon, capelin
and then there was the cod because the cod followed the capelin
the bait, right? Clockwork

Here at the end of Herring Cove Road, Shoal Bay, Fogo Island
I can walk right into your paintings
the old fish store, the salt box houses
This one's Aunt Sadie's
grand old soul, knitting in the rocking chair by the stove
I sold Aunt Sadie mats for her floors
And this one, the old fella who lives in the white house in Barr'd Islands
He's 92, his wife's there, too

Here at the end of Herring Cove Road, Shoal Bay, Fogo Island
you paint old sharemen, caps turned just so
fishing cod traps with nets and forks
in trap skiffs and punts
suspenders hold up baggy green pants
back straight as the dip net they're hauling with
Was never any good at painting faces

It was the hardest work, the less paid work
and the best work I've ever done in my life

Here at the end of Herring Cove Road, Shoal Bay, Fogo Island
I paint what I know, I paint what I see
I paint what's here

I know if I painted anywheres else
I'd still be painting stages

Winston Osmond is a painter and jack-of-all-trades from Shoal Bay, Fogo Island, Newfoundland and Labrador.

SO IT BEGINS AT HASTINGS BAY

for Don and Frances Kay

Looking to buy land
in the woods
on the edge
of remote

she takes you to Hastings Bay

dreary day
grey sky
light rain

She points to the hill
What do you think of that place, for a house?

You say
Do I have to get out of the car?

Yes, she says
Come on, she says
Look, she says

Following her arm
you see dimpled-skin bay
circles encircling circles

A faint sheen of sound nuzzles your ear
and the bay becomes your staff
the water pocks your notes

The wind's tendrils the stems
and its gusts the flags

the silver the sustain pedal
that holds it all together

to make this little dance of rain for flute

You turn, counter-clockwise
pause, at nine o'clock
woods still
but then a puff, a wriggle
as air gentles a leaf
Music for an image, another round
you turn: six, three, then back to twelve and nine
notes collide

Fired by these images
you make sound collages
of red and blue
warm in fulsome summer
cold in barren places

The spaces between the highs and lows
layer colours to mirror the contours
and textures of raw rugged land
and a heart laid bare
in tune with the scapes of your birth
—sound, land, sea—

A rondo for your island
Tasmania

Don Kay is an award-winning composer and music educator who lives in Taroona, a suburb of Hobart, Tasmania.

WHEN YOU COME IN LATE TO AN ISLAND

for Adam Young

When you come in late to an island
and the party's in full swing
it's not love at first sight
(well it is)
but it's also hard living
not in a box
hard getting used to seeing the horizon all the way round
losing yourself
uncluttering

When you first come in to the island you think
oh god you're in Gander
gotta go gotta go gotta go
got an hour-and-a-half drive to the ferry in Farewell then
got an hour ride on the ferry to Stag Harbour
(and you hope it's not combined)
and then you get to Fogo Island and you go
gotta drive gotta drive gotta drive
You're a reluctant islander here in Shoal Bay
and every now and then you go squirrely
need your fix of family, Walmart, Costco, the mall
beer with your buddies
gotta leave gotta leave gotta leave

But three years in on this island
you don't think about time anymore
(well you do, you're a teacher and a husband and a dad, after all)
but at least you can stop and take a breath
gotta breathe gotta breathe gotta breathe
A calm comes over you
as you drive to the ferry
and you cross on the ferry
and you're home safe
in the net of your ocean

You say you don't know if you need a barrier around you these days
(but you guess you do
since you find yourself painting it all the time)

On the front porch of the island you watch the sun go down
catch right-out-of-the-tube colour from the sky
and swirl it onto your canvas
markers and pencil crayons and airbrush and spray paint

and wind like a thousand horses
bending the windows of your house
to your breathless
gotta paint gotta paint gotta paint

Especially the fishing stages
witnesses to decades of rain, salt, tides, and ice
Their spindly legs, crooked grins, zany hats
a jaunty tilt of the roof, smile in the lilt of the door
a twinkle in the window of an eye

At night you hear them wake up
take a walk around the island
splash through harbours, high-dive off cliffs
cavort with seagulls, play hopscotch on rocks
They make it safe home by morning
(most of the time)

Lately they've taken to showing up on your doorstep
hiccupping and hungover
sheepish and a little contrite
so you reel them in to your canvas
and paint yourself into the party
gotta stay gotta stay gotta stay

Every now and then this island washes over you
the interconnectedness of the people and the land and everything
you guess it's from the stages
that crossing of the threshold that gives them life

You say this island's the house that you sleep in at night
gotta dream gotta dream gotta dream

Adam Young grew up in Moncton, NB, and moved to Fogo Island with his wife Jennifer who was from Joe Batt's Arm. They live in Shoal Bay with their children. Adam teaches in the school and paints whenever he can.

BENDING LIGHT

for Hillary Younger

People have certain misconceptions about photography, about what it does and what it is. One of them is that we try to represent reality. In a sense that's right. But in a sense it's completely not right. Because what we're actually trying to represent is memory.

—HILLARY YOUNGER

Where sea meets land
land meets trees
trees meet mountain
mountain meets air
Where warm tones meet cool
where the edge of light meets the lie of the land
where blue meets sea and shore
you get wet stuff

Like when you've been out in the bush for a week
taking pictures morning and night
You sense the life in the place
the time, mood, pace
You feel it
You put away your light meter and read it with your body
Like playing an instrument so well you don't think about the notes
You just play it as you feel it
Try and catch it with your lens
and transmit where it gets you
really really deep

That mix of light and motion
Painting with light
Holding back light
What you search for
what you strive for
is remarkable light
Then you find something earthbound to match it

But part of you goes into right brain
so that all that you're seeing is shapes and light
and lines and shapes
and how they're all reacting
and the way that reacts with film is magic

You tell me how
the sun pokes above the horizon
or from under a cloud
or behind a rock
and you get this little sliver of bright sun
caught in your lens
it goes *thwang*
Sun star

Or the story of the dodgy track
in the dark with your head torch on
You shinny down the cape
to the sea ledge
Sea storms in under the cliff
the waves haul in in sets
You know about rogue waves
the ones that kill fishermen
You read them
'til the timing is right
then jump to the next ledge
I might get my feet wet, but that's all right
The shot's the thing

But this wave
doesn't splash your feet
It breaks over you and tries to sweep you out
You hang on to your camera and the tripod and the edge

of the ledge
I'm inside the wave it's on top of me I can't breathe
water everywhere and then it's gone

The stolen hotel shower cap
still covers your lens
And as you drink your lungs full
you think

I wonder if it still works

Hillary Younger is a wilderness photographer who lives in Tasmania when she's not taking
award-winning photos of the world's wild places.

5

FINDING HOME

JUST BECAUSE YOU COME FROM AN ISLAND

for Doug House

Growing up
you never thought that much about the island
about being a Newfoundlander

But off to school in Montreal and Toronto
and later teaching in Calgary
you'd hear the jibes
silly jokes about me, our people

You tell me the story of a party where somebody says
Oh, I heard this great Newfie joke
Then he looks at me and he says
You don't mind, do you, Doug?
And I say, Yes, I really do mind
The room goes quiet
You could hear a pin drop
Then somebody changes the subject

You tell me the story of your colleague who asks you
to do a guest lecture about Newfoundland
You say, *Yeah, sure,* then you realize
Just because you come from a place doesn't mean you know it
You read up, enough to bluff your way through

You tell me the story of coming back
for a job teaching Newfoundland culture
on educational TV, travelling the island
interviewing Joey Smallwood, Richard Cashin
You become steeped in it, loyal to it
know that if you are going to make a contribution
you want it to be here
Be part of Newfoundland's own quiet revolution
where people like Cabot Martin and Brian Peckford
started questioning the '60s aspirations

to get an A&W or Kentucky Fried Chicken franchise
to catch up to mainland Canada or the rest of the world
It was like we had given up on Newfoundland identity
that thoughtless headlong rush into modernism
by which you do what other people do

You tell me a story
about your father growing up
in the 1920s, '30s, when Newfoundland
was a country
How, when he said, *heading to the west coast*
he meant Corner Brook

You say
just because I came from Newfoundland
didn't mean I was a Newfoundlander
It only happened
when I came back

Doug House is a St. John's author and sociologist who taught for many years at Memorial University and served in a number of senior positions in the province's public service.

PART OF THE CONVERSATION
for Danielle Wood

As a child you were the magpie
picking up the shiny bits of family lore
and hoarding them against the day
you would need them

With *should I stay or should I go?*
pounding in your head
you left to write your novel
in the corrugated iron shed in Broome
the far north of Western Australia

Miserably homesick, unbearably hot
you cooled yourself with stories of home
where you could walk the streets with your mother and uncles
who'd known everyone since they were children
who was married to who and
who was not married to who anymore

Soaked in this big community memory
with the idea that what you do
will never go away
Not many things happen that many people are outside of
When the bridge fell down, everybody knew somebody
who was either on the bridge, or got stuck in traffic

But you could not bear being out of earshot
that home was going on without you

Tasmania
the place where mountain and water make sense
where the light falls differently
and where you can be the kind of person who sees
the difference

I like knowing what my patch is.
I like knowing I can walk that far
and if I go any farther
I'll be off the edge
This is the patch on which I can play out my life
be part of the conversation, whatever it is

Even when you left
you were always coming home

Danielle Wood is a writer, journalist, and academic who lives in Tasmania. Her books include Mothers Grimm, Housewife Superstar, *and* The Alphabet of Light and Dark, *which won the Australian/Vogel Literary Award in 2002. She also writes under the pen names Minnie Darke and Angelica Banks.*

ROCK OF THE HEAD

for Michael Mooney

Oliver's Cove calls you to
its jagged jut at the end of the road
past slant pole fencing
that careens around gardens turned for winter
tuft-topped root cellars
and the abandoned barn
home of the town's last pony

Through hummocks, gulches, and knolls
the music of the sea jangles your veins
draws you like the salt-water blood of fishers
who know the names of every rock and tickle
Sweeney's Gulch, The Raggedy Nuddick
Tickle of the Head, Rock of the Head
every washing pond where sky pools
and clouds shimmer through old glass windows
gaze unwavering past Pigeon Island
to the lops on the sea

Back snug into the island's spine
you watch waves as big as Tilting's houses
groundswells from yesterday's storm
grind against the head's rocky teeth
beyond reach of the needling spray
you listen, take it in

Your canvas a soundscape
layered with deep bass booms
the slam on rock
clack of stones and screels of gulls
shriek and keen of wind
bellow and wail of tide
the song of the ocean here long before you
it will sing on long after you're gone

You catch a few of its waves
a haunt that fills your nights

Fingers mellow guitar strings
wind on the marshgrass twists
the ribbon of your vocal cords
as you sing us back
to the sea

Michael Mooney is a singer-songwriter whose father's family is from Prince Edward Island and his mother's from the island of Montreal. He lives in Charlottetown.

THE LIGHT AT UNCLE ART'S

for Zita Cobb

You didn't know it at sixteen
watching contrails write the road to away
that even before you left
you were on your way home

You didn't know it at sixteen
as you dreamed of travelling the world
that the light at Uncle Art's house would stay lit for you
because on this rock in the Labrador Current
a lot of lights have gone out
and it's always nicer to see a light coming into the harbour
than a light leaving

You didn't know it at sixteen
that the boat you sailed
would become your house, your island
Every inch of it, I knew it well
Through every storm at sea
I depended on it
When you attach that deeply
to a boat, to an island
your capacities as human beings
come awake
When you move away from the edge
whether it's the boat, the island, the bigger island
and finally you're in Toronto,
how do you know who you are?

You didn't know it at sixteen
that Uncle Art's house would become *your* house
eight-hundred-square-foot salt box
contains every single bit of space
you need to live a life

What's here has a place
If I want to introduce a new spoon
that requires some consideration
It offers all kinds of potential
because I don't get distracted

You didn't know it at sixteen
that you'd end up shorefast to this place
as sure as a cod trap moors to the shore

You only know where you are
when you're on the edge

Zita Cobb grew up in Joe Batt's Arm, Fogo Island. She is the creator, with her brothers, of the Shorefast Foundation, the Fogo Island Inn, and other social enterprises on Fogo Island.

EVERYTHING RETURNS, EVENTUALLY...
for Frank Ledwell

Wrecked boats, messages in bottles, lifebuoys, jetsam, fishermen lost at sea.
—JOANNE HARRIS, *Coastliners*

You would like that I'd remembered
flatter than piss on a plate
to describe the Bay at sunset
when the wind drops
and, becalmed
you take up your deck chair
pour two fingers of The Captain
sneak another smoke
and watch the sun
slip day's net

As violet night comes down
you bide your time
waiting to hoist your sail
for that last short leg to home

Frank Ledwell (1930–2010) was a writer and poet who mentored thousands of Prince Edward Islanders—including me—in his role as English and Creative Writing professor at the University of Prince Edward Island.

Dr. Laurie Brinklow teaches in the Master of Arts in Island Studies program at the University of Prince Edward Island. She is particularly interested in the power of place and story, and their impact on island identity. She is the author of *Here for the Music* (Acorn 2012).